Singsong Crows and Alphabet Soup

KaZ Akers

Dedication:

To my son, Jack, and my husband, Todd, for your unwavering support and unconditional love. You are my best teachers. I learn something from you every day.

Acknowledgements:

My unending love to these kind, compassionate and unparalleled individuals:

Josie DiVincenzo, Merry Simkins, Dipika Patel, Ute Elmer, Heike Peter, Leni Sloan, Dale Janda, Linda Hough, Nora Lott, Kurt Engstrom, Yvonne Woo, Allen Wong, Maggie Wong, Meryl Newbern, Joe Bonelli, Lucio Munoz, Rev. Dr. Karen Langford, Hong Yuhe, Steve Kimelman, Bill Roman.

You keep me moving forward by inspiring and supporting me.

My sister, Kara. Thank you for...well, you know.

To our beautiful but fragile planet for feeding me every single day, every single hour and every single minute.

Poet's Note Dada Poem: Dada combats traditional ways of thinking and creating. It is expressed in music, writing, sculpture, painting, photography, puppetry, and more. Dada came into being around 1914 as a protest against the first world war, and is attributed to Tristan Tzara and Hugo Ball, among others. It was influenced by Cubism, Expressionism and Futurism. What appear to be nonsensical words and phrases are up for interpretation and are best read aloud. For me, there is no attachment in Dada and Dada composition is pure artistic freedom. Spontaneity and absurdity are encouraged. Dada's resurgence can me heard in the music of Cirque du Soleil and from David Byrne and Talking Heads.

All Original Poetry: KaZ Akers

Cover Design: Jack Akers-Brownlee

Photographs: KaZ Akers, Todd Cruse

Photo Editing: Jack Akers-Brownlee

Special thanks to: Dr. Karunesh Kumar Agarwal (Managing Editor) Cyberwit and Taj Mahal Review for helping make one of my dreams come true.

This book is my love letter to life.

I write directly from my observations and life experiences.

The poems are jovial, sad, exuberant, angry, content, quirky, defiant and determined.

Just like life.

Thank you for reading.

I hope you find something that resonates with you.

Love,

KaZ

Contents

I Am Not Invisible

I am not invisible.
I am skin and bones.
Flesh and feelings.
I am tooth and nail.
You exist because I exist.
Experiences from chosen and inherited exploits.
I may be grey but I cannot be red-lined.
I still move with sinewy precision in mind and body.
Your jokes and taunts deter me not.
The rubbish heap of your generational prejudice
holds no sway to my determination and grit.
Maturity is an art form.
I'm past knee-jerk and conclusions jumped to.
Time may be on your side but infinite patience is on mine.
I've seen the outcomes of decades of decisions.
Fair weather fragments fade into indelible brain tangles.
Let's not speak of lessons learned but of lives lived.
Each to their own lessons.
Flailing youthful energetic enthusiasm transitions.
When you laugh at me you laugh at yourself twenty years
hence.
The evolution of existence has been cherry-picked to elevate
early essence.
Paths are forged by previous participants.
We are the building blocks of our predecessors...
and our successors.

When It's Hardest

Lift up, not tear down.

Rise above.

Be the extended hand.

Express the encouraging word.

Navigate the rocks like swift moving currents.

Effortlessly flow over and around.

Erect a door in the wall.

When it's the hardest

love the most.

Lift up, not tear down.

This

The setting sun
as a backdrop.

The brilliant red, pink, orange
painted across the sky.

Lying atop the hill
in the cool grass.

Warm air, cool air,
warm air, cool air
swirled all around.

This peace.

This contentment.

This.

I Believe In People

I believe in people.
I believe people can bring out
the worst and the best in each other.
I believe people change.
People carry loads.
People move mountains.
They feed the hungry,
clothe the poor,
educate the ignorant,
heal the sick,
comfort the suffering,
bury the dead.
People laugh.
People cry.
They cheer and lament.
We as people
appreciate,
critique,
revere and respect.
We the people,
all the people,
are what makes
the world,
the universe,
the cosmos,
and the infinity of space
go 'round.

Life of Extremes

Living a life of extremes
will not center us,
will not bring us peace.

Being on one side
or the other of the path
will not center us,
will not bring us peace.

Traveling straight down
the middle of the path
will not center us,
will not bring us peace.

Embracing the fullness
of yin and yang equally
that will center us,
that will bring us peace.

Inescapable

Whatever you name it:
cause-and-effect,
karma,
consequence,
what goes around
comes around
it is inescapable.

Whatever walk of life
you come from,
whatever you believe,
or don't believe
it is inescapable

Whatever you radiate
you attract.

Flowing Like Water

See the person you desire to be,
gracefulness, peace, bliss.
Flowing like water.
The ethereal living in human form.
In the moment.
Flowing like water.
Day by day,
radiant and resplendent.
Flowing like water.
The agenda to live life with ease.
Whatever comes passes through
and transforms into liquid.
Flowing like water.
Navigating the rocks
and the limbs.
Untethered by the weights we carry.
Flowing like water.
Flowing like water.
Flowing as water.

Enough

Today
I woke up.

Alive
and
well.

That is enough.

Forgot

Living in the world

finally forgot your face,

your smile, and your voice.

What is Possible

I have sat with the possibility
of what is possible,
probable,
likely,
and improbable of it all.

I have found strength,
fortitude and -
if truth be told -
the peace of it all.

The unasked questions answered.

The asked questions unnecessary to ask.

Good Guy, Bad Guy

I like the good guy
who is kind of a bad guy,
and the bad guy
who is kind of a good guy.

I want to watch a good guy
who is really bad,
and he's good at it.

Sometimes, though, the bad guy
is bad at being bad.

But when he's good,
he's surprisingly good.

It Is

Is is, isn't it?
Is it not is
or is it?
It is.
It is it.
Or is it it?
Is is,
and is is not.
Is is not is.
Is not not is?
Is it?
Oh yes, it is.

Let Go of Your Hate

Don't let the haters
make you a hater.
Hating haters is just as hateful
as haters hating.
Hate today and you will hate tomorrow.
Haters hate movers and shakers
so move it and shake it
and leave the hating to the haters.
When you start hating
hating is hard to stop.
You may end up hating yourself for hating.
(You see where I'm going?)
Hate does not stop with hate,
it starts with hate.
In the end
it's not hating your hate
that lets go of your hate.
It's loving the hate out of your hate
that lets go of your hate.

The First Appearance

The first appearance.
Chill in the air.
The purity of each little flake
as it tumbles from the sky
and lands in perfect formation
on the ground.
The absent signs of trudging
through each icy sculpture.
Snow sits on top of the distant mountain
like a monument to winter.
A chilly wind navigates under my scarf
and brushes my neck with frigid kisses.
Wayward flakes settle on my eyelashes
and melt into icy tears on my cheek.
The crackling flurries under my new boots
pierce the silence.
Glacial air feels jubilant.

Clever Little Minx

Grab me by my shoulders
and shake me.
Shake off my humorlessness.
Snap me out of my worry.
Bring me back to joy
and a sense of wonder.
Show me the laughter and reverie.
Help me to ignore stupidity,
and release obligation.
Shine so I may see
the futility and ridiculousness.
Pull me out of this endless loop.
Barrage me with silliness and hilarity.
Too long have I been wrenched by my hair
believing versions of stories that are not mine.
Instead I turn my head to the skies
and cackle at myself.
Tickle me with your quips and jest.
No more to drag myself
through the mud of disappointment and despair.
Clever little minx
taking my role too seriously.
Playing the fool when I am
the jester manipulating the sovereign.

Overestimated

I overestimated your smile.
I overestimated your warmth,
and the touch of your hand.
The laughter,
the lessons,
the smells dancing through your kitchen.
I overestimated the sound of your voice.
Of his voice.

Then your picture hanging on my wall
fell and shattered.
His voice forever silenced.
Your voice now absent like
an expected letter that never came.

Through it all I questioned how I would endure
without your smile,
your warmth,
the tinkling of the tea cups,
the ringing of champagne flutes.

How I would endure
without the sound of your voice,
the smells in your kitchen.

Eventually it all dimmed,
and I realized
I had underestimated myself
by overestimating you.

Challenged

Those who seek peace
are always
challenged
by those
who seek power.

Tara Ratata - A Dada Poem

Ichiidoon kabata
oré ichii noon

Ichiidoon katata
oré nashi zoon

Tara ratata
Tara ratatata
Tara ratata
Tara ratatata

Ahn mogley tata harung
Zara zara oh gishinoon

Ah zo beetay
eetay
Zazo beetay

Ah zo beetay
eetay
Zazo beetay

Tara ratata
Tara ratatata
Tara ratata
Tara ratatata

Alla alla allay
eetay
alla alla allay

Alla alla allay
eetay
alla alla allay

Ichiidoon kabata
oré ichii noon

Ichiidoon katata
Oré nashi zoon

Aray, arayaray

Aiyay

Aray, arayaray

Aray, arayaray

Aiyay

Aray arayaray

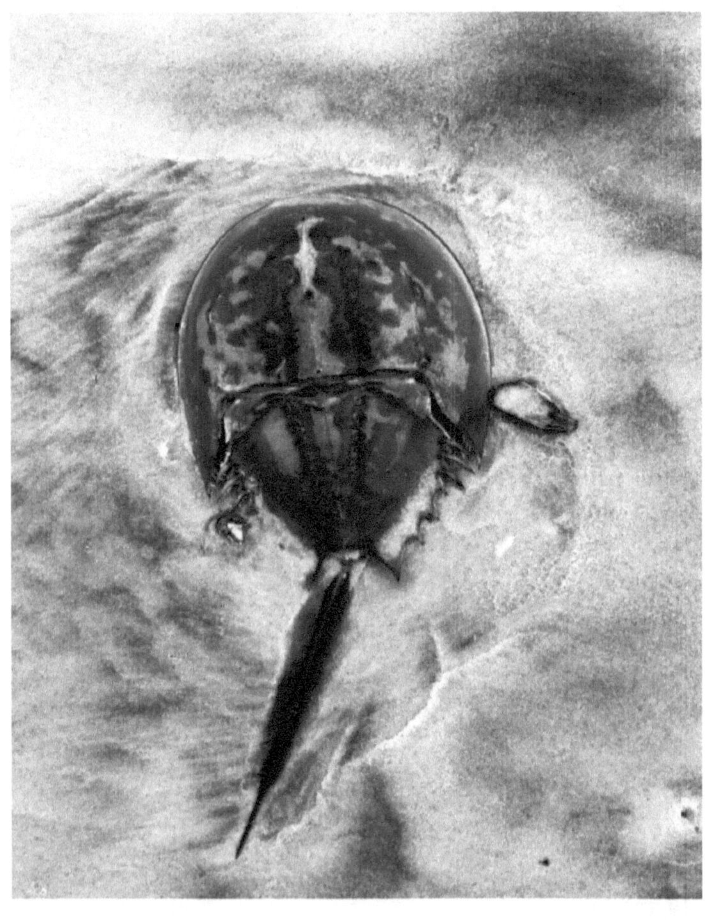

Writing

I don't find writing
so hard.
I simply stare
at a piece of paper
until it eviscerates me
and
I spill my guts
onto it.

Too-Tight Jumper

It tore at the seams like a too-tight jumper.
The one you now struggle to get over your head
and feels binding at the chest.
The threads unraveled at the cuffs and collars.
No amount of stitching will rescue this jumper.
You look at it like a long lost lover
that no longer fits in your life.
The wool feels soft and warm but then again
it annoyingly scratches your neck.
You can't wait to remove it.
It's harder to remove than it is to pull it on.
Desperate to remove it and all the while
aching from the loss.
One last glance and you slip it into a donation bag.
Perhaps someone else will benefit from what you've outgrown.
A scratchy jumper that at one time felt like a lover's kiss.
Now it feels like a hangman's noose.
One you cannot escape quickly enough.

Life's Too Damn Short

We have to do
the best we can do
without getting wrung out
by continually navigating
people.

We have to be
the best we can be.
Accept it,
address it,
or abandon it.

Life's
too
damn
short.

Through A Fisheye Lens

We walk around with one eye shut.
Seeing what may or may not be.
Through a kaleidoscopic lens
with a myopic view.
We exist with no peripheral vision.
Creating proverbial hallucinations.
If we look does that mean we really see?
Life through a fisheye lens.
Through a convex lens.
These eyes, trusting our purview
with one eye shut to the world.

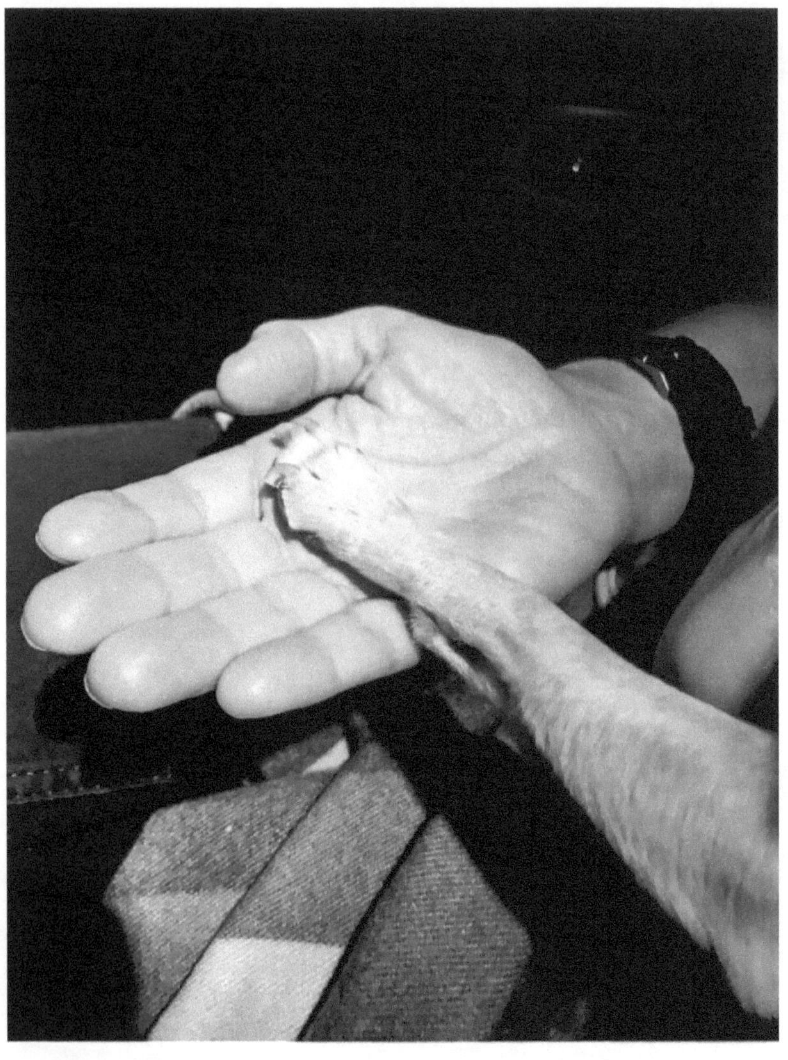

Hate Not

Hate not on this day.
For hate shall follow you home
and remain your guest.

The Porch

I've recently read stories
about African-American families
and life on the porch.

Porches were a safe zone,
the children's "do not pass" zone
when mothers needed a break.

Places for family connection,
for neighbor to talk to neighbor,
for kids to play.

The front porch would catch the night breezes.
If you were lucky enough to have a porch swing
you could coax those breezes
swinging back-and-forth, back-and-forth.

I read those stories with a smattering of envy.
Time spent on a front porch.
A joyous time of gathering.

I have fond memories of front porches.
Mine were not memories of closeness and community.

Indeed, my southern grandparents
and great grandparents
had big front porches.
You could fit generations on each porch.
You could, but we never did.

Save one rare occasion when five people

sat and posed for a photograph
on the steps of great grandmother's front porch.

Daddy,
Granny,
Mom (my great grandmother),
Mrs. Painter (my great, great grandmother)
and me.

That yellowing photograph
is tucked away somewhere.
A once-in-a-lifetime occurrence.

Each porch had a moving diversion.

An enormous glider on one,
where I'd smoothly coast all day long.

A hearty, floating swing on another.

I would swing so hard, with such abandon,
it would smack the bannister behind it.

Hitting the bannister was immediately followed
by great grandmother running outside and bellowing:

"Stop hittin' the railin', young lady!"

Turning on her heels, she'd jerk the screen door handle,
stomp back into the house, screen door slamming behind her.

On rare occasions "Mom" would sit for a few fleeting moments,
sharing a glide with me.

She would talk of her asthma and how lonely she was
since the early death of my great grandfather.

Typically, everyone was too busy to sit and swing.

I learned to love the solitude of a glide, a swing.

My other companion was an old fashioned tricycle.
Not much of a friend, but a friend nonetheless.

I pestered Daddy into carrying it up
the never ending wooden steps leading from the cellar.

This tricycle sat patiently at the foot of the porch stairs
waiting for me to ride after my daily swing.

This particular tricycle had an enormous front wheel
and two tiny back wheels.

Between the back wheels was an iron platform.

Another person could stand behind me and be my passenger.

I don't recall ever having one.

I'd barrel down the sidewalks pretending to be anywhere but there.

Inside the house with the porch swing it was always noisy;
a television and arguments loudly played all day.

Smelly cigarette or pipe smoke wafted through the air.

Across town, at the house with the glider,
I played the piano.

It sounded dreadful since I only pretended to play.

"Close that piano and go outside!"

I was bored anyway.

I tumbled through the front door,
and curled up on the glider.

Oftentimes, I'd walk through the narrow backyard
amongst the pristine rows of hybrid roses.

I'd stand at the edge of the yard,
near the creek that separated me
from the train tracks.

Waiting patiently for a train to pass
I'd skip rocks across the "crik",
just like grandfather taught me,
and do my best not to tumble in.

Without fail the train engineer waved to me
and blew the shrill whistle
as the engine passed.

The summer brought barrels full of green apples
bursting from the trees.

I'd climb high in the tree and eat my fill.

Granny stood on the back porch
chiding me for eating crabapples
insisting they'd give me a "bellyache".

They never did.

During my visit I'd be sent to the neighbor's
to retrieve fresh picked raspberries.

"Mr. and Mrs. Nelson" always seemed glad to see me.

They talked about their grandchildren,
or gossiped about people I didn't know.

They gave me hard candies filled with jelly,
always offering more for me to stuff into my pockets.

I kept them a secret because too much candy would "rot my teeth".

Secrets were a family tradition.

Porches were never a gathering place.

They just kept me occupied.

They became a place to live in my imagination.

A place to pretend,
to dance,
to sing,
and swashbuckle.

Whiling away the hours and weeks of summer vacation,
my porches taught me to appreciate my own company.

I lived like the whole world was mine...

on the porch.

Skin Of Each Other's Skin

The line between laughter and lunacy,
between pain and joy,
between the here and the there,
does not exist.
There is no line.
These things co-mingle and co-exist.
Splendid and sorrowful
gives rise to creation, to creativity.
They are hand in glove.
They walk together,
sometimes silently,
sometimes boisterously.
They sip sweetened and bitter tea
and find that neither lacks.
They each contribute to themselves.
Once must survive so the other can be.
More than yin and yang,
it's skin of each other's skin.

Spoken Too Hastily

Overly ambitious weathering of metaphors,
catchphrases and buzz words.
Leaping from prosaic,
to rhyme, to colloquialism.
Intertwining different forms,
structures and motifs
that do not flow freely
from one to another one.
Spoken too hastily
causing worlds to run together.
So arduous to understand.
Rampant verbal gesticulation
imitates performance art,
in turn, distracting from the words.

Nothing Left To Transcend

Never going to get there.
Never going to have the answers.
Time to stop asking,
seeking,
searching,
examining.
Does it matter?
To explain the inexplicable.
To query,
contemplate,
capitulate.
AND...
if you get answers, does it matter?
Everything is still as it is.
What do you seek to understand?
There is no next because
next brings you back to start.
With answers gratification is fleeting.
Then wanting more, more, more.
This is it.
The waiting is now over.
Seeking involves more interrogation.
When there is no longer a question,
when there is no longer a yearning,
when need for resolution ceases,
we have arrived.
Nothing left to transcend.

Dance With Adam Ant

When I grow up I won't grow old.
I'll grow strong.
I'll grow bold.
I'll say thank you when you say something nice.
I'll smile, flip my hair
and won't think about it twice.
It's fine to be humble.
Humble is allowed.
Humble keeps you grounded
with no need to please the crowd.
I've got to say that yesterday
I downplayed my worth.
Nothing wrong with loving
our talents by birth.
Jealousy and envy may have gotten you down.
Just keep doing what you are doing.
It's worth it,
stick around.
We take it all so seriously
and serious doesn't last.
Grasping, groping, numbing, doping
is a check you can't cash.
Ask me what I want
there won't be a rant.
Honestly, it would be lovely
just to dance with Adam Ant.

No Harm

Do me no real harm
for I wished no harm on you.
Nonetheless, harm done.

Who I Am

I know who I am.
I thrive in
the here and now.
I know what
I need to know,
when I need
to know it.
Banded with hearts
across the continents.
I am me, just me.
Wearing the human label.
Standing tall
amongst the reeds
and the willows.
No obligation
to words salads.
In full view
without obstacles.
Unshackled from the
tyranny of sameness.
Unbounded by the
tribalism of belonging.
Joined to the
community of being.

Marauding My Dreams

Finally stopped being in love
with what we were.

A memory.
A fantasy.
So long ago.

Years,
and places,
and people ago.

Roads diverged after the intensity
and ecstasy of discovery.

No limits.
Love full out in the blush of youth.
Burning so hot.
Both it scorched.

All this time
a flash,
in a dream,
in a vision.
It disturbs my sleep.

It makes little sense.
I am only a shadow of she.
You are only a memory of he.
A lifetime ago.

After so many roads,
experiences.
So much time,
distance.

It's just an illusion,
a fantasy of what was.
What is no more.

Marauding my dreams.

Oh, Life!

Oh, life!
with thine
vexatious sting.
Tarry not
'neath the shadow
of the Snow Moon
solely to chill
mine own heart
and break my spirit.

Real, Honest Love

Love is not blind, it is clear sighted.
Love is intelligent.
Love is honest.
Love must sometimes be firm.

Honest love is painful.
Honest love expresses itself non-violently.
Honest love knows alternatives.
Honest love is transparent.

Real love is compassionate.
Real love is accepting.
Real love takes a deep breath.
Real love is unconditional.

Real, honest love makes itself known.

What Do I Want For You, My Son?

What do I want for you, my son?

I want you to be a citizen of the world.

I want you to experience all this world has to give you.

To accept and acknowledge your shortcomings,

and develop and increase your strengths.

Love yourself for the beauty that is in you.

Make mistakes and learn from them.

Listen to your intuition,
then trust yourself.

Those who wish to be in your life will stay.

Nurture them.

There is no need for bad friendships
or those who consume the life out of you
and leave you hollow.

Bequeath your legacy to the wind,
the trees, nature and the ethers.
Let it expand through time.

Be like bamboo:
bend in the wind and rain,
sustain life,
stand tall
and be stronger with other bamboo.

Singsong Crows and Alphabet Soup

Hapless replicants succumb
to the emotional face-slapping
of their most adored.

Too young to think for themselves.
Growing up as lip-synching Stepford children.
Unable to realize the word welding.

Lacking the option to think for themselves.
It's knee-jerk singsong crows cawing.
It's alphabet soup.

Little mimics basking in the glow
while drowning in the rain of
a ritualistic onslaught.

Victims of an explosion in their synapses
hurling them off a cliff
and splattering into the gorge
of their blown minds.

www.ingramcontent.com/pod-product-compliance
Lightning Source LLC
Chambersburg PA
CBHW030959180726
47993CB00018B/1176